Yorkshire

from

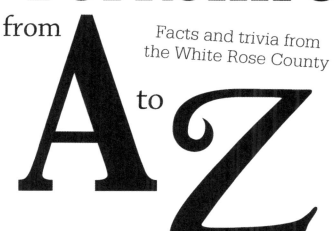

Facts and trivia from
the White Rose County

to

From **a**le to **z**ebra crossings!

Written by
Adrian Braddy

Dalesman

Published in Great Britain in 2017 by Dalesman
an imprint of
Country Publications Ltd
The Water Mill, Broughton Hall, Skipton BD23 3AG
www.dalesman.co.uk

© Adrian Braddy 2017

Additional material © copyright holders as stated 2017

ISBN: 978-1-85568-365-5

All rights reserved.

Printed in China by 1010 Printing International Ltd

Contents

Introduction

Putting together this little book has been an absolute joy.

Since I first considered compiling a Yorkshire A to Z I must confess to having had some reservations. "Will the format be too restrictive?" I pondered. "And what about the prickly problem of the letter Z?"

In the end I needn't have worried. As soon as I began jotting down ideas and eking out snippets of trivia from my overloaded bookshelves, I realised the format actually encouraged variety.

The alphabet took me to unexpected new areas, introduced me to new facts, and revealed – if there was ever any doubt – the vast diversity of this county's landscape and heritage.

It gave me an excuse to bring together the unlikely bedfellows of the boomerang and the zebra crossing, combine earthquakes with fairies and pair up underwear and vampires.

Hopefully you'll find a surprise on every page – some facts you'll know, a lot you won't. There are achievements, inventions, foodstuffs, sports and festivals, plus the occasional piece of completely useless, utterly marvellous, Tyke trivia.

Please join me on an adventure through Yorkshire from A to Z.

Adrian Braddy

A is for ale

"The world's best ale comes from Yorkshire" declared the *Spectator* magazine in 2016, and it would be churlish to argue.

The brewing of ale has been carried out in the county for centuries and Yorkshire has become famous the world over for its fermented malt and hops.

Until the dissolution of the monasteries, brewing was controlled by the church. The Cistercian monks of Fountains Abbey, North Yorkshire, brewed sixty barrels of strong ale every ten days in a malt house measuring sixty square feet. At the time, ale would be consumed with all meals, as there was no tea or coffee and it wasn't advisable to drink water.

In the modern era, Yorkshire's thirst for ale is stronger than ever. Now real ale is back in vogue across the United Kingdom, Yorkshire is home to at least eighty breweries, both large and small. According to the Directory of UK Real Ale Breweries, the county produces almost a third of the UK's beer.

Landlord, the pale ale made by Keighley's Timothy Taylors, has won more awards than any other beer in the country.

It is also worth noting that the device used for serving up a foaming pint of ale was invented by a Yorkshireman. Joseph Bramah patented the beer pump in 1784.

A is for AEROPLANES

Long before the Wright brothers made their first tentative flights, a Yorkshireman named George Cayley had successfully designed and built a working, piloted flying machine.

Cayley, from Brompton-by-Sawdon, near Scarborough, is known as the father of aeronautics. He is also considered by many to be the first person to understand the underlying principles and forces of flight.

He first set forth the concept of a fixed-wing flying machine in 1799, identifying the four forces of weight, lift, drag and thrust. These discoveries are central to modern aeroplane design. He was also the first to create and utilise cambered wings, a distinctive part of aircraft to this day. He even, in effect, reinvented the wheel in his quest to make his aircraft lighter. His light-tension wheel was a forerunner of the modern spoked bicycle wheel.

In 1804, he flew the first successful unmanned glider of which there is any record.

Above: George Cayley; Opposite: a replica of the Cayley flying machine at the Yorkshire Air Museum; Below: Cayley's original design

Cayley, from Brompton-by-Sawdon, near Scarborough, is known as the father of aeronautics

Then, in 1853, after years of design and research, an unnamed man – probably a member of Cayley's staff or possibly his grandson – became the first adult aviator when he flew across Brampton Dale in Cayley's glider.

Another pioneering Yorkshire aviator was Amy Johnson. Born in Hull in 1903, she became the first woman to fly solo from Britain to Australia. She was aged just twenty-six. Up until that point the furthest she had flown was from London to Hull. Unsurprisingly, she became a global hero and thousands greeted her on her return to British shores.

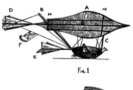

Fig.1

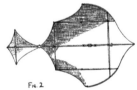

Fig.2

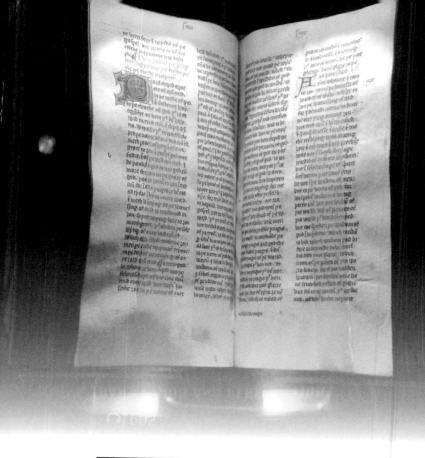

Above: an original John Wycliffe Bible

B is for *Bible*

The historic county of Yorkshire has more acres than the Bible has letters. There are 3.8 million acres in the county, compared with 3.6 million letters in the Old and New Testaments.

That we are able to read the Bible in English – never mind count the letters it contains – is thanks to a Yorkshireman. John Wycliffe produced the first English-language Bible manuscripts back in the 1380s. With the help of many followers and scribes, he penned dozens of translated copies of the scriptures, translating them from Latin.

In 1415, years after his death, Wycliffe was declared a heretic. The Pope ordered his body be exhumed and his bones burned. His ashes were cast into the River Swift in the English Midlands.

Wycliffe's legacy was long-lasting. Being instrumental in the development of a full translation of the Bible, he made the scriptures accessible, for the first time, to laypeople.

In 1535, fellow Yorkshireman Myles Coverdale produced the first complete printed translation of the Bible into English.

A detail from the Wycliffe Bible proclaims, in Middle English, "In the beginning was the word, and the word was at God..."

B is for battle

Generations of schoolchildren know the date of the Battle of Hastings is 1066, but how many have even heard of the Battle of Towton?

This conflict, fought almost 400 years later on Palm Sunday 1461, during the Wars of the Roses, deserves to be far better known.

The battle is almost certainly the largest and bloodiest ever fought on English soil. More than 50,000 soldiers from the Houses of York and Lancaster fought for hours in horrible conditions. An estimated 28,000 lost their lives on the battlefield. As a result of the carnage, which took place near the tiny village of Towton, North Yorkshire, the Yorkist Edward, Duke of York, took the crown from Lancastrian King Henry VI.

The Battle of Towton imagined in a woodcut of the 1920s

B is for boomerang

You may associate boomerangs with the Aboriginal Australians, but according to one of Britain's best-known authors, this distinctively shaped throwing device may actually have originated in Yorkshire.

Terry Deary, writer of the *Horrible Histories* series of children's books, made the claim after jogging on Ilkley Moor, in West Yorkshire.

His evidence is a mysterious carving, said to be 3–4,000 years old, which has baffled experts for centuries. The Swastika Stone (pictured below) carries a five-armed symbol in the shape of a swastika.

"It's the earliest representation of a boomerang," he said. "There is nothing else it could be."

He added: "The ancient Britons had the weapon in 4000BC, long before the aborigines made it in Australia. The Britons used the boomerang to kill birds and small animals but not sabre-toothed tigers or mammoths."

Deary's claims were not well received Down Under. "The Aussies are hopping higher than kangaroos over this," he admitted.

C is for Christmas

The origins of many key elements of a modern Christmas and New Year can be traced back to Yorkshire.

It is said that Britain's first Christmas festival was celebrated by King Arthur in York in AD521.

In his *History and Description of the Ancient City of York* (1818), William Hargrove wrote that in "521, this great monarch, and his clergy, with all his nobility, and soldiers, celebrated, in this city, the nativity of Christ – not by holy conversation but in the spirit of heathenish revelry, with feasting and mirth; in wantonness and many excesses… This was the first Christmas festival ever held in Britain; and hence our present custom originated".

For most people the turkey is the

Yorkshireman William Strickland is said to have introduced the turkey to Britain

centrepiece of the Christmas dinner and for this tradition also, Britain has Yorkshire to thank. This bird, native to the Americas, was said to have been introduced to England by William Strickland of the East Riding of Yorkshire. It is claimed that Strickland acquired six turkeys as part of a trade with Native Americans during an early voyage there in 1526. He brought them back and sold them in Bristol market for tuppence each.

He is said to have continued trading in turkeys, eventually making so much money he was able to build a stately home in Boynton, near Bridlington.

Strickland adopted the turkey as the family crest in 1550 and the drawing of his coat-of-arms is thought to be the earliest depiction of the turkey in Europe.

The village church, where Strickland was buried, features several representations of turkeys, including stained-glass windows, stone sculptures and a carved lectern.

Meanwhile, there was great consternation north of the border in 2014 when *The Scotsman* reported: "Research suggests Hogmanay originated in Yorkshire".

The New Year festival is much beloved of Scots but the newspaper broke the news that: "new etymological research shows that the earliest citation of the word is found not in Scotland, but a few hundred miles south in – whisper it – Yorkshire".

A household accounts ledger from 1443 contains the first recorded instance of the word. The document is part of the estate of Sir Robert Waterton, of Methley, West Yorkshire, whose family were trusted servants of the House of Lancaster.

In it, Sir Robert's household manager describes payments for a large "hogmanayse" and a smaller "hogmanayse", references to gifts of food.

At the time, Hogmanay was a word shouted by children as they went from door to door in search of treats and gifts during the New Year period.

Another Christmas tradition, now almost entirely extinct, has rather more irrefutable Yorkshire roots. The Yorkshire Christmas Pie was a lavish pie stuffed with all sorts of game and boned birds. A giant Yorkshire Christmas Pie, which required four men to carry it, was served at Windsor Castle in 1858.

C _is for_
cat's eye

There have been many great British inventions, but few can have saved as many lives as the "cat's eye". Invented by Halifax-born Percy Shaw in the 1930s, the cat's eye remains a staggeringly ingenious piece of design, even by modern standards. The story goes that Percy had his eureka moment while driving home to Boothtown through Queensbury one dark and densely foggy night. Spotting a sharp reflection in the beam of his car headlights, he brought his

vehicle to a standstill. On stepping out of the car, Shaw discovered that the reflection came from the eyes of a cat crossing the road on an evening prowl. More importantly, he found he had been travelling on the wrong side of the road and had he continued on a straight path he would have plummeted over the edge of the twisting roadway. Shaw, like many motorists in Britain at the time, had relied at night upon the reflections of his headlights on tramlines set into the road to safely guide them home. The emergence of buses and the subsequent demise of the tram led to the removal of tramlines, a move that unintentionally made the roads a much more dangerous place. This remarkable sequence of events is the most famous account of the invention, though it is also said that reflective studs on street signs were Percy's true inspiration.

Whatever it was that inspired him, Percy was quick to put his creative mind to work. And what a mind it was.

From a young age, Percy was regularly coming up with new ideas and problem-solving inventions. He was one of the few in Halifax to own a car and his love of everything mechanical gave him an interest in repairing all kinds of vehicles.

He ran a small business laying asphalt drives and paths, and he developed a motor roller that speeded up the task immensely, giving him an edge over his competitors. Once he had the idea of creating a cat's eye road-stud, Percy set about perfecting the design. Dedicating much of his spare time to the idea of a night-time driving guide, Percy came up with numerous draft designs. After many trials and failures, he came up with a winning concept – an iron shoe sheathed in rubber, implanted with a glass reflector.

In 1934 he patented the design, complete with self-cleaning mechanism; the rubber coating, soaked in rainwater, would wipe the reflectors clean whenever a car drove over the stud. Simple yet brilliant, Percy's cat's eye went on to be voted the greatest design of the twentieth century, although it was a long while before the authorities could be persuaded to invest in its development. In March 1935, Reflecting Roadstuds Ltd was incorporated, with Percy Shaw as managing director, and for the rest of his life the development of the cat's eye was to occupy most of his energies. The usefulness of the design was finally recognised by government during the blackout of the Second World War, and Percy's cat's eyes were, for the first time, widely adopted across the country's road network. The company continued to grow after the war and by the 1950s, it had its own iron foundry, a rubber-processing factory and a glass-manipulating plant, giving it manufacturing independence. A decade later it expanded into the overseas market and in 1965, Percy was awarded an OBE for services to export.

A famous television interview with Alan Whicker saw Percy become a household name, but he continued a reclusive lifestyle. Despite being a multi-millionaire, he never left the home his parents had moved into when he was two years old. As Whicker discovered, he had removed all the carpets and curtains, living in a virtually bare room.

An early advertising poster for cat's eyes, under Shaw's brand name "Catseye"

The cat's eye remains an ingenious piece of design

The room did, however, contain three TVs. They were always on; one tuned to BBC1, the second to BBC2 and the third to ITV. He died on 1st September 1976 at the age of eighty-six, but to this day his cat's eyes are still saving lives on roads around the world. Thanks to this amazing legacy, both Percy Shaw and his greatest invention are true Icons of Yorkshire.

Did you know?

Percy Shaw started work as a labourer in a cloth mill aged thirteen

D is for drystone walls

Much of the landscape of the Yorkshire countryside is made up of a patchwork of fields stitched together by walls built from stone, without cement. Indeed, Yorkshire has more drystone walls than any other part of the country. According to the Countryside Agency, the county has approximately 18,900 miles (30,420km) of drystone walls – more than a quarter of England's total. If stretched end-to-end, they would reach three-quarters of the way around the equator.

D

is for

Devil's
Arrows

Each day, thousands of motorists drive close by the Devil's Arrows without even realising it. The three towering standing stones stand in an almost straight line, virtually parallel to the A1(M) as it passes Boroughbridge and crosses the River Ure. The largest of the pillars measures 22 feet 6 inches (6.8m) in height, making it England's second-tallest standing stone.

Legend has it that the Devil fired the giant millstone grit "arrows" at nearby Aldborough, but missed, almost striking Boroughbridge instead.

Above: a blue plaque at the site dates the Devil's Arrows to c. 2700BC; Opposite: one of the standing stones

The largest of the pillars measures 22 feet 6 inches, making it England's second-tallest standing stone

In reality they are said to be part of a larger Neolithic network of stones that also includes the Thornborough Henges, close to Masham.

There were once four, or perhaps even five, stones at Boroughbridge. In his *Britannia*, first published in 1586, historian William Camden stated that one "was lately pulled down by some that hoped to find treasure there, though they sought in vain". It is thought that part of the fallen stone was used to form the support of a nearby bridge.

E is for *earthquake*

In 1931 the Yorkshire coast was rocked by the strongest earthquake ever recorded in the UK. The Dogger Bank quake measured 6.1 on the Richter scale. Its epicentre was located 60 miles (97km) off the coast in the North Sea, meaning damage caused was significantly less than if it had centred on the mainland.

The effects of the Dogger Bank earthquake were felt as far away as Belgium and France

In Filey, the church spire was twisted by the vibrations. In Hull a number of chimney stacks crashed to the ground and patients in the city's Royal Infirmary woke to the "violent rocking of their beds", according to the local paper. One elderly woman in Hull died of a heart attack, apparently brought on by the shock. In Bridlington, a policeman fell from his bicycle and at Flamborough Head, parts of the cliffs crumbled away.

A small, non-destructive tsunami wave was also reported to have hit the Yorkshire coast.

The Dogger Bank earthquake began at about 1.30am on 7th June 1931, and lasted about twenty seconds. The effects were felt as far away as Belgium and France. Damage was reported in seventy-one places.

In London the tremors caused the head of the Madame Tussauds waxwork model of Dr Crippen, the murderer, to fall off.

E is for Easter

If you've ever wondered why the date of Easter moves about from year to year, the answer can be found in Yorkshire. Back in AD664, at Whitby Abbey, a meeting of church leaders – the Synod of Whitby – was held. As a result of the discussions, King Oswiu of Northumbria decreed that clerics should follow the Roman tradition of Easter, rather than that used by the Celtic church. Ever since, Easter has been a moveable feast.

In recent times, the world's major churches have suggested Easter should be held on a common date each year, but the idea has not gone down well in Whitby.

A traditional Pace Egg Play in Heptonstall, West Yorkshire

According to the *Whitby Gazette*, Councillor Joe Plant said: "The procedure has been in place for centuries – why change it? It would be disrespectful to Whitby. If it isn't broken why go about trying to change it?"

The town's mayor, Councillor Heather Coughlan, was quoted as saying on the subject: "Whitby jealously guards its history and heritage, of which the Synod and Captain James Cook are a major part. I don't think it necessary to interfere with something which has worked well for 1,400 years and I'm sure the people of Whitby will take the same view."

Easter was historically celebrated with great gusto in Yorkshire – but there were no chocolate eggs in sight.

Instead paste or pace eggs were popular. In 1876 John Harland noted that hard-boiled eggs were colourfully decorated and used for games. "The eggs are first boiled hard with some coloured preparation, pink, yellow, and so on, marked, if you like, with the owner's initials.

"On Easter Monday and Tuesday, at Whitby, a fair is held in the space between the parish church and the abbey, when children assemble to roll or 'troll' eggs in the fields adjoining."

Egg rolling (or trolling) was popular in many parts of the county, particularly the North and East Ridings. Another tradition was "jarping" or "jawping" of hard-boiled eggs in a game similar to conkers.

In his book *Yorkshire East Riding* (1951), John Fairfax-Blakeborough explains the rules:

"Holding a hard-boiled egg in the clenched fist with the point only visible in a circle formed by the thumb and index finger, the challenge was given, 'I'll jarp tha!' There was then a trial of strength of egg-shells to see which could stand the impact."

To this day a traditional Pace Egg Play is performed in parts of West Yorkshire, including Heptonstall and Midgley, every Good Friday.

Easter was also a time for feasting. Harland said: "This festival is marked here by the extensive consumption of custards, baked at the public ovens in 'dubblers', or large dishes."

Another speciality at this time of year was the simnel cake. *Chambers's Journal* of 1907 stated: "Scarborough is specially the home of the simnel-cake, although other Yorkshire towns produce them."

F is for *fairies*

"**W**hen you have eliminated the impossible, whatever remains, however improbable, must be the truth". These are the famous words of the great detective Sherlock Holmes. So when the creator of one of literature's most rational, level-headed characters is confronted with photographs purporting to show fairies, you'd think he'd discount them out of hand. Yet Sir Arthur

The first photo, "Frances and the Fairies"

Conan Doyle took the pictures of the Cottingley Fairies as unquestionable proof of the existence of winged sprites.

The photographers of the Cottingley Fairies were two young girls, Elsie Wright and her cousin, Frances Griffiths, who said they had regularly seen the fairies around the beck near the West Riding village of Cottingley, near Bingley.

"The recognition of their existence will jolt the material twentieth century mind out of its heavy ruts in the mud"

Elsie borrowed her father's camera and took the most famous picture of Frances with the "fairies" (previous page). Five photos were produced in total: two in 1917 and a further three in 1920.

Doyle, a spiritualist, believed and used the photographs to illustrate an article he had written for the Christmas 1920 edition of *Strand* magazine. It sold out within two days. Of the fairies, Doyle wrote: "The recognition of their existence will jolt the material twentieth century mind out of its heavy ruts in the mud, and will make it admit that there is a glamour and mystery to life."

Elsie and Frances finally confessed to the hoax in the 1980s, admitting the fairies were in fact paper cut-outs of pictures copied from a children's book.

In a 1985 interview on Yorkshire Television's *Arthur C. Clarke's World of Strange Powers*, Elsie said that she and Frances were too embarrassed to admit the truth after fooling Doyle, the author of Sherlock Holmes: "Two village kids and a brilliant man like Conan Doyle – well, we could only keep quiet." In the same interview, Frances said: "I never even thought of it as being a fraud – it was just Elsie and I having a bit of fun and I can't understand to this day why they were taken in – they wanted to be taken in."

But, despite repeated investigations proving all the pictures were faked, Frances always maintained they had seen the fairies and insisted the fifth and final picture was genuine.

F is for football

The crest of Sheffield Football Club carries a proud boast: "The world's first football club". Founded in 1857, Sheffield FC created the first official set of football rules, the Sheffield Rules, which provided the basis for the rules of the modern game.

Sheffield FC created the first official set of football rules

Three years after the birth of Sheffield FC, near neighbour Hallam FC was formed, allowing the two clubs to play the world's first official football derby. To this day, games between the two sides are known as the Rules Derby. In 1867 Hallam won the world's first ever football tournament, the Youdan Cup.

Sheffield Football Club's crest, proclaiming it to be "the world's first football club"

G is for ghosts

York is said to be the most haunted city in the world. According to a survey of paranormal activity by the Ghost Research Foundation International, a total of 504 spirits have been recorded there – more than in any other city. Jason Karl, patron and co-Founder of the GRFI, said: "Although I remain an arch-sceptic I admit, I have seen more things go bump in the night in York than any other city I have visited in the world."

The Guardian reported in 2011 that "York is teeming with ghosts – even M&S is haunted", adding "there are almost as many ghost walks in York as there are ghosts". A whole industry has sprung up around the ghostly goings-on within the city walls.

Some of the more colourful (in character, if not in complexion) ghosts roaming York's historic streets include the Headless Earl and Mad Alice. The body of the Earl of Northumberland, executed for

Above: the headless ghost of Thomas Percy, the seventh Earl of Northumberland, is said to haunt the area around Goodramgate; Opposite: it is claimed 35 Stonegate is home to at least fourteen ghouls

treason in 1572, is said to be regularly seen near Goodramgate, fruitlessly searching for his missing head. Mad Alice has haunted Lund's Court, between Swinegate and Low Petergate, since she was hanged in 1825.

Meanwhile, the seventeenth-century Ye Old Starre Inn is apparently haunted by an old lady dressed in black, a number of soliders, and even two black cats often sighted near the bar. The felines were said to have been bricked up inside a pillar between the bar and the door – an old Yorkshire superstition meant to protect against bad luck. Records show the cellars of the pub, which are much older than the current building above, were used as a makeshift hospital for soldiers during the Civil War.

York's most haunted building, however, is said to be 35 Stonegate. The current building dates to 1482, though there has been a house on the site for many more years than that. At least fourteen different ghosts are believed to haunt number 35. It has been speculated that renovation work in the 1990s stirred the souls from the walls.

G is for gunpowder

Y orkshire's – and perhaps Britain's – most notorious villain is Guy Fawkes. Born and educated in York in 1570, Fawkes converted to Catholicism and fought in the Eighty Years' War

Bates

Robert Winter

Christopher Wright

Iohn Wright

on the side of Catholic Spain. On his return, he joined a group of plotters planning to assassinate King James I and restore a Catholic monarch to the throne.

The leader of the 1605 Gunpowder Plot, as it became known, was not Fawkes but Robert Catesby, yet it is Fawkes whose name has become synonymous with the plot, and whose effigy is, to this day, burned on bonfires every 5th November.

Fawkes is remembered because he was the plotters' gunpowder specialist. It was he who was to have lit the fuse on the barrels of explosives stockpiled in an undercroft they had leased beneath the House of Lords. Following a tip-off, it was Fawkes who was found standing guard over the gunpowder and it was Fawkes who, after being tortured, eventually confessed to the plot. He was spared the extended agony of execution when he fell from the scaffold where he was about to be hanged and broke his neck.

A contemporary engraving showing some of the Gunpowder Plot conspirators

Guido Fawkes

Robert Catesby

Thomas Winter

is for

Hornblower

The watch has been set in Ripon every night for more than 1,100 years. At 9pm each evening the Wakeman of Ripon sounds a note on a horn. It is an extraordinary ritual that dates back to Viking times.

The original horn was given to Ripon in AD886 by King Alfred the Great. Having recaptured London from the Norse invaders, he toured the country, boosting the confidence of his people. Particularly impressed by what he saw in Ripon, he granted a Royal Charter to what was only a small settlement, presenting residents with a ceremonial horn – the Charter Horn – which survives to this day.

The King advised Ripon folk they should remain vigilant at all times if they wanted to maintain their good quality of life and so it was decided to appoint a Wakeman. This individual would stay awake through the night, patrolling the area from dusk till dawn. He would announce the start of his shift by sounding the horn.

Although the dangers of Viking invaders have long since passed, the tradition remains, albeit with a new horn. Ripon continues to appoint a Wakeman and the hornblowing ceremony can be witnessed at the Ripon Obelisk.

Ripon is not the only Yorkshire town with an ancient hornblowing ceremony.

The blowing of the Bradford horn took place for hundreds of years. It dates back to medieval times when John of Gaunt, the Duke of

Lancaster, gave land to John Northrop for killing the Boar of Cliffe Woods. On 11th November each year this would be marked by three blasts of the horn in the marketplace by a man accompanied by a hunting dog. The boar was the stuff of local legend and it was said to have terrorised Bradford until a reward for its capture was raised. The legend is enshrined in the Bradford coat of arms, which is topped off by a boar's head.

In York Minster's Treasury can be found another ceremonial horn. The Horn of Ulf is one of the few surviving artefacts from the beginning of the eleventh century. Intricately carved from an elephant tusk in Salerno, Italy, it belonged to the Viking nobleman Ulf, or Ulphus, who owned large estates around York and throughout Yorkshire. As with the Bradford horn, the Horn of Ulf acted as land deed. It remains in remarkable condition for its age.

In the village of Bainbridge, Wensleydale, drinkers at the Rose and Crown can see the village horn in a case on the wall. Although rarely sounded these days, for centuries the horn was used as a guide for travellers who had got lost after dark in the wilds of the Wensleydale forest.

Until recently, generations of the Metcalfe family sounded the horn at 10pm every evening from Holyrood (27th September) to Shrovetide (the day before Ash Wednesday).

The Wakeman's House, Ripon, was once the official residence of the Wakeman or hornblower

Did you know?

To pay the Wakeman, a tax was levied on the citizens of Ripon based on which way their house door faced – houses with doors facing the market square or a main thoroughfare were considered wealthier and charged four pence per year, compared to a penny for those less well-off

i is for *inflatables*

O f the many things Yorkshire has brought the world, perhaps the most bizarre is the inflatable football crowd.

The opening scenes of hit film *The King's Speech* (2010) take place at Wembley Stadium, where in 1925 the future King George VI gave a halting, disjointed speech that first brought his stammer to public attention.

Because Wembley has since been completely rebuilt, director Tom Hooper looked to West Yorkshire to recreate that famous scene. Elland Road, home of Leeds United, doubled for Wembley, along with Odsal Stadium, base for the Bradford Bulls.

Hooper had previously filmed at Elland Road, which was used as a location for *The Damned United* (2009). "Because I'd shot there, I knew it was one of the few remaining period stadiums that look like the old Wembley," he said.

As the budget was low, there was no money to hire thousands of extras to fill

Above: Colin Firth and Helena Bonham Carter as the future George VI and Queen Mother in *The King's Speech*; Opposite: inflatable extras fill the stands at Elland Road. Photo courtesy of the University of Huddersfield – fashion students from the university helped to dress the dummies

the stadium seats. Instead, producers brought in 1,500 inflatable mannequins from the Inflatable Crowd Company, based in Bingley, West Yorkshire. The unlikely-sounding business was set up to supply life-size plastic dolls for film productions.

Company director, former Bingley Grammar School student Danny Burraway, explained after filming, "We create the mass, while the real extras, placed in front of the inflatables and intermingled throughout, provide the life by moving or cheering."

According to *King's Speech* graphic designer Amy Merry, blow-up people are far more convincing than computer-generated figures.

"They look very funny when they arrive. They came in period costume because they'd already been used for *The Changeling*. But once they're put in the seats and inflated, they look great."

Real-life extras, including a number of soldiers, were used for the close-up scenes where Colin Firth made his speech.

J is for *jet*

If you own a piece of Whitby jet you are lucky enough to possess something of almost unimaginable age. The jet found on this part of the North Sea coast dates from the Early Jurassic era, and is approximately 182 million years old.

Whitby jet, deemed to be the finest in the world, is wood from a species similar to the Monkey Puzzle tree that has been compressed over the generations until it becomes fossilised.

It is possible to polish jet to such an extent that it could even be used as a mirror, which led to its popularity as a decorative item.

The demand for Whitby jet soared when Queen Victoria wore jewellery made from the gemstone in remembrance of her beloved Albert. It soon became good etiquette to wear jet while mourning.

By this point, there were some 1,500 people employed in the jet industry and Whitby had several dozen workshops dedicated to fashioning the gemstone into beautiful jewellery and intricate carvings.

K is for King Arthur

The location of Camelot, King Arthur's castle and court, has for centuries been the subject of fevered rumour and speculation, but there is a growing belief that Camelot was located not in Cornwall, Wales or Scotland, but in the South Pennines, near Huddersfield. And that King Arthur, therefore, was a Yorkshireman.

Gustave Doré's illustration of Camelot for Alfred, Lord Tennyson's, *Idylls of the King* (1868)

Professor Peter Field, a world-renowned expert on Arthurian literature, says Camelot was a small Roman fort at Slack, to the west of Huddersfield.

In Roman times, the fort at Slack was called Camulodunum, which means "the fort of the god Camul". Over the years, the professor theorises, well-recognised linguistic processes would have reduced Camulodunum to Camelot.

This site at Slack would have been considered a strategic stronghold in Arthur's day. At that time, the invading Anglo-Saxons had occupied much of the east and south coasts of Britain, but Celtic-speaking Britons held the north and the west coast. The natural gathering point for Britons who wanted to resist the Anglo-Saxons would have been Chester, and the point that they needed to hold, if they were not to lose the entire east coast, was York. Slack is on the Roman road from Chester to York, but the location was no less strategic for that.

In Roman times, the fort at Slack was called Camulodunum. Over the years, this would have reduced to Camelot

Prof Field explained: "If there was a real King Arthur, he will have lived around AD500, although the first mention of him in Camelot is in a French poem from the Champagne region of France from 1180. There is no mention of Camelot in the period between those dates, known as the Dark Ages, when the country was at war, and very little was recorded. In this gap, people passed on information, much got lost in transmission, and people may have made up facts or just messed up known information."

Fellow Arthurian writer Simon Keegan agrees that King Arthur was from Yorkshire. In his book, *Pennine Dragon*, he explained: "Arthur's father Mar was the King of York (Ebrauc) – he even took the name Uther (Iubher), meaning York. Therefore we should not be surprised to find Arthur's legendary castle nearby."

K is for Kiplingcotes Derby

What is believed to be the oldest horse race in England takes place in the East Riding village of Kiplingcotes every spring. It has to be held, whatever the weather (and it's often pretty inclement), because the rules state that if ever the race does not take place then it must never be run again.

During the famously harsh winter of 1947, a local farmer ensured the future of the race by leading one horse around the course. During the 2001 foot-and-mouth crisis, the race was again reduced to just a single horse and rider.

First drawn up in 1519, the rules are delightfully eccentric. They decree that the prize money for coming second can be more than for winning the race. Riders must weigh in at ten stone excluding saddle. The entry fee in 1619 was four guineas and that's how it remains. The clerk is still paid five shillings (25p) each year to administer the event.

Publicity means the race is as popular as ever these days, with up to 1,000 people turning up to enjoy this quirky piece of English history.

The finishing post for the Kiplingcotes Derby, proclaiming it to be "England's oldest horse race"

$\mathcal{L}$ is for leeches

The village of Aiskew is pretty unassuming. Despite its appearance in the Domesday Book, it has long been – to outsiders at least – in the shadow of its near neighbour, Bedale. Beside Bedale Beck, which separates the two communities, stands an unusual brick-built building that may well be the only one of its kind still standing in Britain. To the casual observer this diminutive, square-shaped, castellated structure serves no obvious purpose; it may have battlements but it is certainly no castle.

As a nearby information panel explains, this is the Leech House, a relic of Yorkshire's rather gruesome medical past.

Built in the late eighteenth century, it is a rare example, as the name suggests, of a store for medicinal leeches, which were used by doctors to treat all sorts of ailments by "blood-letting". Leeches are a type of worm which have a front sucker that draws blood from the body.

One British medical text recommended blood-letting for acne, asthma, cancer, cholera, coma, convulsions, diabetes, epilepsy, gangrene, gout, herpes, indigestion, insanity, jaundice, leprosy, ophthalmia, plague, pneumonia, scurvy, smallpox, stroke, tetanus, tuberculosis, and about one hundred other diseases.

Doctors and apothecaries kept the bloodsuckers in "leech jars", which were often surprisingly ornate

Above: a leech jar; Opposite: The Leech Finders by George Walker (from *The Costume of Yorkshire*, 1814)

Given the Leech House's location, it is presumed the leeches were sourced from the beck.

In *The Costume of Yorkshire* (1814), George Walker illustrated Yorkshire's "Leech Finders" at work.

The text accompanying the plate states, "Leeches are now so much in demand that they are comparatively scarce, though still found in many parts of Yorkshire. The women who collect them are principally from Scotland, and

41

though by no means the fairest of their sex, are notwithstanding by no means disagreeable subjects for the pencil.

"Their dress has some peculiarity in it, and they promenade bare legged with considerable picturesque effect, in the pools of water frequented by leeches. These little blood suckers attach themselves to the feet and legs, and are from thence transferred by the fair fingers of the lady to a small barrel or keg of water, suspended at her waist."

Doctors and apothecaries kept the bloodsuckers in "leech jars", which were often surprisingly ornate, and Yorkshire had a thriving industry making these.

Hartley, Greens & Co, the Leeds pottery, which exists to this day, was making leech jars from cream-coloured earthenware from around 1780 onwards. Similar wares were manufactured at Castleford pottery, founded by David Dunderdale in 1790.

It is just possible that the Aiskew Leech House was the source of leeches used to treat a patient at nearby Pickhill in March 1818.

The incident was recorded in the diary of Benjamin Newton, Rector of Wath in the Dearne Valley. He wrote: "Rode to Pickhill with Anne and Mrs Newton, and the former this morning (20th) complained of a violent shivering before we went to Church... on coming from Church we found her alarmingly ill and immediately sent for Dr Whaley who gave her a dose of calomel with salts and

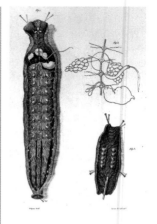

Above: diagram of a medicinal leech; Opposite: the leech house, Aiskew, North Yorkshire

senna which however seemed to yield no relief to her head which continued most excruciating and she was scarcely relieved this morning (21st) when three leeches applied to her temples seemed to give a slight relief. Dr Whaley came at one and applied eight more which seem to take off the pain from her head." The following day, Newton returned from church to hear that "my dear Anne was more improved than Dr Whaley could have expected." The leeches, it seemed, had worked their magic.

The use of leeches peaked between 1830 and 1850, then fell out of fashion towards the end of the nineteenth century thanks in part to the invention of mechanical leeches, and changes in medical methods. As a result, Aiskew's Leech House would have become redundant.

By the mid 1980s, when it became a Grade II listed building, the Leech House was in a derelict condition, missing most of its battlements and with its triangular-headed windows blocked up. However, a team of volunteers from a local heritage trust restored it to its current state – though they didn't bring back any of its wriggly bloodsucking residents.

M is for mills

For many, William Blake's description of the "dark satanic mills" is their enduring view of Yorkshire. For a time, at least, the county was the weaving capital of the world, with giant mills dominating large swathes of the urban West Riding. At their peak, wool amounted to a quarter of all British exports.

Yorkshire's mills experienced a dramatic decline and fall, and only a small number remain. However, of those that do, a number thrive and continue to lead the world.

Above: Armley Mills in Leeds, once the world's largest woollen mill, now houses an industrial museum; Opposite: Salts Mill in the model village of Saltaire, near Bradford, is now an art gallery

For a time, at least, the county was the weaving capital of the world

One of the most famous, A W Hainsworth of Stanningley, has a proud history dating back to 1783.

At the Battle of Waterloo, the British battle lines, known as the "thin scarlet line", were scarlet thanks to Hainsworth's bright red fabric.

In 1918, the distinctive blue uniform of the RAF was supplied by Hainsworth.

Both Prince Charles and Prince William wore Hainsworth cloth at their weddings.

And the iconic bright red uniforms of the Queen's Royal Guards are famous the world over thanks to Hainsworth fabric.

Did you know?

Due to the rapid rise of the textile industry, the population of Bradford grew by 50% every ten years between 1811 and 1851

M is for mousetrap

A sk anyone the world over to visualise a mousetrap and they will almost certainly bring to mind the same design: the wooden platform; the coiled metal spring; the sort of thing that appeared so often in *Tom and Jerry* cartoons invariably attached to the tail of a squealing Tom.

Its purpose may be gruesome but its design is one of the most enduring of all time and it remains instantly recognisable. Even now, 120 years later, it is estimated that the Little Nipper, as it is called, accounts for sixty per cent of the world's mousetraps.

Designed by Leeds ironmonger James Henry Atkinson in 1897, the design of the Little Nipper has remained almost unchanged ever since.

The trap was first made by Procter Brothers Ltd in 1897 and Atkinson sold the company the patent in 1913 for £2,000.

The creative Atkinson patented various inventions during his life, including a number of mousetrap mechanisms, but none matched the Little Nipper.

Its ingenious yet lethal design shuts in 38,000s of a second – a record that has never been beaten, according to the makers of the trap.

A mousetrap very similar to James Henry Atkinson's 1899 wood and wire Little Nipper design

M is for Mother Shipton

Supposedly born during a thunderstorm in a cave on the banks of the River Nidd in Knaresborough, North Yorkshire, in 1488, Ursula Southeil would become England's most famous prophetess.

According to accounts of her life, her mother was aged just fifteen and her father nowhere to be seen, so Southeil was raised in the cave. It is claimed that although she moved into more suitable accommodation at a fairly young age, she would return to the cave later in life, preferring to live away from neighbours who mocked her odd habits and strange appearance.

One biographer described her as "very morose and big boned, her head very long, with very great goggling, but sharp and fiery Eyes, her Nose of an incredible and unproportionate length, having in it many crooks and turnings, adorned with many strange Pimples of diverse colours, as Red, Blew, [sic] and mixt, which like Vapours of Brimstone gave such a lustre of the Night, that one of them confessed several times in my hearing, that her nurse needed no other light to assist her in the performance of her duty."

From the cave, Mother Shipton, as she became known, made remedies and potions from the herbs and leaves she found in the forest. She made a living from selling the potions, and also from predicting the future.

After her death, the legend of Mother Shipton intensified, and since the mid-seventeenth century more than fifty editions of books about the prophetess and her predictions have been published.

The great diarist Samuel Pepys, as London burned during the Great Fire in 1666, recorded: "See – Mother Shipton's word is out."

Mother Shipton

Above: an engraving of Mother Shipton; Below: Mother Shipton's house; Previous page: Mother Shipton's Cave

"In water iron then shall float, As easy as a wooden boat"

One edition of her prophecies predicts the end of the world. "The world to an end shall come/In eighteen hundred and eighty one."

It also contains the lines: "In water iron then shall float, As easy as a wooden boat."

However, the true author of the book containing these prophecies, which did not appear until 1862, subsequently admitted it was a fabrication.

Mother Shipton's Cave and the nearby petrifying well have drawn curious visitors since 1630, making it England's oldest visitor attraction.

is for

Nobel Prize

The neighbouring West Yorkshire boroughs of Kirklees and Calderdale have, to date, produced an incredible six Nobel Prize winners. To put it into context, that's more than Brazil, Bulgaria, Kenya, Latvia and Iceland combined.

Owen Willans Richardson, of Dewsbury, won the Prize for Physics in 1928. He worked in the field of thermionics and his name was given to the law of physics connected to his research.

In 1951, Todmorden-born John Cockcroft picked up the Prize for Chemistry along with colleague Ernest Walton. The duo are credited with being the first to successfully split the atom.

Fellow Tod native Geoffrey Wilkinson received the Prize for Chemistry in 1973, along with Ernest Otto Fischer.

Todmorden's John Cockcroft, above, and colleague Ernest Walton are credited with being the first to successfully split the atom

Halifax-born John Walker jointly picked up the Prize for Chemistry in 1997 in recognition of his research into DNA.

He was followed in 2007 by another son of Halifax, Oliver Smithies, who received the Prize for Physiology or Medicine.

And in 2010, Robert Edwards, of Batley, won the Prize in Physiology or Medicine for research into reproductive medicine.

The neighbouring West Yorkshire boroughs of Kirklees and Calderdale have produced an incredible six Nobel Prize winners

Yorkshire has been the birthplace of a further three Nobel laureates.

Bradford's Edward Appleton was awarded the Prize for Physics in 1947 for his discovery of the ionosphere. George Porter, of Stainforth, South Yorkshire, received the Prize for Chemistry in 1967 for his research into chemical reactions. And Nevil Mott of Leeds shared the Prize for Physics in 1977 for his work into the electronic structure of magnetic and disordered systems.

Owen Willans Richardson of Dewsbury won the Prize for Physics in 1928 and his name was given to the law of physics connected to his research

N

is for

naked

Visitors to Settle, North Yorkshire, cannot fail to notice an eating place with a decidedly odd name – Ye Olde Naked Man Café. The name of this former inn, which dominates the high street, comes from a figure carved in stone on the building's walls. The carving appears, at first glance, to show a naked man, with his modesty only spared by a board carrying the date 1663 and the initials "I C".

The name of this former inn comes from a figure carved in stone on the building's walls

Above: the Naked Man, and, below, the Naked Woman

Ian McMillan once amusingly described the image as resembling "the kind of key you might get in a downmarket hotel".

On closer inspection, it appears the

man is not naked at all, as tunic buttons, sleeve-ends and stocking tops can still be made out.

However, despite this, when Queen Victoria visited the market town, it is said the Naked Man was "completely obscured" to avoid any embarrassment.

At Langcliffe, just a few miles north, there was also said to once be a Naked Woman Inn, named after another stone carving, engraved "1660 LSMS". So just three years separate the naked duo.

A number of theories and legends have been put forward to explain the Naked Man. In his 1972 book *It's Odd, It's Yorkshire*, Arthur Gaunt suggests the sign refers snidely to the fact that Settle folk were noted once for an absence of sartorial pride.

The name Naked Man may have been used to poke fun at the Quakers

Another theory suggests the man is, in fact, lying in a coffin, suggesting the building was once home to an undertaker, or that someone was buried there in 1663. It has also been advanced that the carving was a satire on fashion or a protest against local taxes, which included paying a halfpenny for the privilege of wearing a new hat to Settle market.

The view of local historian Tony Stephens, who has produced a guide to Settle, is that James Cookson, whose insignia can be seen on the wall, used the name Naked Man to poke fun at the Quakers of the town, at a time when there was discord in Settle between Anglicans and Quakers.

Whatever its origins, the Naked Man has long amused visitors. One high profile fan was the composer Edward Elgar. Close friend Wulstan Atkins was to relate later: "He was excited by becks and waterfalls – and also by the name of your local inn, The Naked Man. It was mentioned in various letters."

According to an article in the *Elgar Society Journal*: "Elgar was fascinated by the Naked Man Hotel in Settle and repeatedly asked Buck [another friend] for a photograph of it, even specifying from what viewpoint the picture should be taken."

is for

Olympics

Team GB's triumphant success at the London 2012 Olympic Games was led by Yorkshire athletes. If Yorkshire were a country it would have finished twelfth in the medal table, with White Rose Olympians bagging seven golds and five other medals. That would have placed it ahead of Jamaica, Spain and the 2016 hosts Brazil. Royal Mail staff across the county were kept busy repainting red letterboxes gold in celebration of the amazing feat. *The Guardian*'s Martin Wainwright joked afterwards: "We can expect a hosting bid from Wetwang in 2020".

In 2016, Yorkshire Olympians did it again, bringing home fourteen medals from Rio, including five golds. Were it a country, Yorkshire would have finished seventeenth that year, ahead of New Zealand, Canada and South Africa.

A gold postbox in Sheffield celebrates the achievements of Yorkshire Olympian Jessica Ennis-Hill

O is for Old Boots

To modern sensibilities, the story of Old Boots sits rather uncomfortably.

Thomas Spence was a humble boot boy at The Unicorn Inn in Ripon who became something of a celebrity thanks to his – to put it delicately – unusual appearance.

Such was his fame that he even caught the imagination of Charles Dickens, who featured him in his magazine, *Household Words*.

Better known as Old Boots, or Tom Crudd, Spence was born with a remarkably long nose and chin which met in the middle of his face.

Seemingly unconcerned by his unfortunate looks, Spence made good money from them. As one Victorian writer put it, "though his singular appearance subjected him to a thousand jokes, yet poor Boots good naturedly bore them all; particularly (which was

Thomas Spence, better known as "Old Boots"

frequently the case) when they were paid for by a present of money."

There have been many vivid descriptions of Old Boots, such as this detailed account from 1808:

"Among the infinite variety of human countenances, perhaps none ever so much excited astonishment and popularity as that of Old Boots, whose portrait has often been engraved.

"This extraordinary person was favoured by nature with a nose and chin so enormously long, and so lovingly tending to embrace each other, that he acquired by habit the power of holding a piece of money between them.

"Old Boots" was born with a remarkably long nose and chin which met in the middle of his face

"Being a servant of the Unicorn Inn in Rippon, Yorkshire, it was his business to wait on travellers who arrived there, to assist them in taking off their boots. He usually introduced himself in the room with a pair of slippers in one hand and a bootjack in the other, exactly in the attitude represented in his picture.

"The company in general were so diverted with his odd appearance that they would frequently give him a piece of money on condition that he held it between his nose and chin. This requisition he was always ready to comply with, it being no less satisfactory to himself than entertaining to them."

Apparently, Old Boots had no problem feeding himself, despite the obvious problem. "On such occasions, the two prominent features of his face were very accommodating," noted one biographer. "By distending his mouth pretty wide, he could contrive at any meal to introduce in a short time a pound of bacon, with a due proportion of bread, beer and vegetables."

Following his death in 1762 at the age of seventy, one publication noted: "He was one of those fortunate beings who could daily accomplish that – which thousands of persons are ineffectually striving all their lives to attain – he could 'make both ends meet.'"

P is for pudding

The first known recipe for a Yorkshire pudding – although in this instance called a "dripping pudding" – appeared in the 1737 publication *The Whole Duty of a Woman*:

"Make a good batter as for pancakes; put in a hot toss-pan over the fire with a bit of butter to fry the bottom a little then put the pan and butter under a shoulder of mutton, instead of a dripping pan, keeping frequently shaking it by the handle and it will be light and savoury, and fit to take up when your mutton is enough; then turn it in a dish and serve it hot."

The original Yorkshire pudding was a stodgy, somewhat thin offering, laden with beef dripping. Its chief aim was to fill you up before the more expensive meat course. Over the last century, the pudding has developed into an altogether different proposition, with the best "Yorkshires" rated according to their height and fluffiness. In 2008 the Royal Society of Chemistry decreed "A Yorkshire pudding isn't a Yorkshire pudding if it is less than four inches tall". It is doubtful if eighteenth-century puddings ever fulfilled this criteria.

P is for pedestrian

I t is often stated that we live in a fame-obsessed world, but the concept of celebrity is nothing new.

In 1762, when Foster Powell left his home village of Horsforth, near Leeds, he had done little to suggest he was destined for fame. He was, according to one account, "a quiet inoffensive lad, shy, and somewhat unsocial, with nothing in the faintest degree remarkable in him, except his fondness for long, solitary walks."

It was this liking for walks that would make Powell a national celebrity. On his death, a book of his life called him the "great pedestrian".

More recently he has been described as "the first English athlete of whom we have any record".

In 1764 he wagered that he could walk fifty miles in seven hours, and won the bet. In 1773 he walked 400 miles, from London to York and back. And in 1788 he walked 100 miles in twenty-one hours, thirty-five minutes. In 1792 he walked

Foster Powell, the "great pedestrian"

again from Shoreditch to York Minster and back in five days fifteen and a quarter hours – almost three hours better than his previous time. The 10*l.* he won for completing this feat is said to have been the largest sum he ever received. He never made any real fortune from his fame and died almost penniless.

In 1764 Powell wagered that he could walk fifty miles in seven hours, and won the bet

At the height of his celebrity, Powell drew huge crowds at the end of his walks. It was said that he drank brandy to sustain him during his long expeditions, also refusing to eat meat.

Physically, he was described as "tall and spare, rather over five feet nine inches in height, very strong about the loins, and with thighs of immense power".

According to contemporary accounts, "his costume was eccentric, consisting of leather breeches and a jacket and a tall hat — about the most uncomfortable garb, one could think … could be devised for a pedestrian".

Although Powell was, according to the *Dictionary of National Biography*, "probably rightly regarded as the greatest pedestrian of his time, or indeed of the century", his achievements were eclipsed during the early nineteenth century. Another celebrated pedestrian, G Littlewood, travelled four hundred miles to Sheffield in 1882 in under ninety-seven hours.

Did you know?

Powell's favourite walk was London to York and back – and it would eventually be the death of him. At the age of fifty-eight, he took it upon himself to attempt to cap his previous best of five days and eighteen hours. He succeeded, completing the walk in just five days, fifteen hours and fifteen minutes – and died soon afterwards at Clement's Inn thanks to his exertion.

P is for prime ministers

The White Rose County has given birth to three of Britain's prime ministers. Charles Watson-Wentworth, the Marquess of Rockingham, was the first, serving two terms, 1765–1766 and again in 1782, after sixteen years in opposition. A member of the Whigs, he was born at Wentworth Woodhouse, near Rotherham.

Yorkshire has given birth to three prime ministers

Above: Charles Watson-Wentworth; Below: Herbert Henry Asquith

Morley-born Herbert Henry Asquith served as Liberal prime minister from 1908 to 1916. He was the last Liberal leader to lead the party in government without forming a coalition.

Harold Wilson, from Huddersfield, was Labour prime minister between 1964 and 1970, and again between 1974 and 1976.

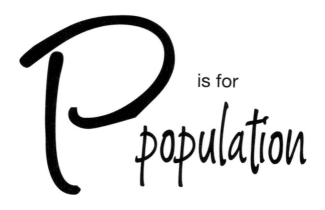

is for

population

Yorkshire just keeps on growing. Estimates suggest that in the 1600s, around 400,000 people lived here. By the time of the first census, in 1801, that figure had more than doubled to almost 860,000. Then, during the Industrial Revolution, the population rocketed. By 1851 there were more than 1.7 million people in Yorkshire and by 1901 that figure had grown to almost 3.5 million.

Yorkshire and Humber has a population of 5,390,576, meaning it is home to more people than Scotland, Wales or Ireland

It is difficult to state with absolute accuracy the current population of the historic county of Yorkshire, as official figures are only given for a region which includes parts of Lincolnshire, and misses out small areas in the North East and North West. However, the Yorkshire and Humber region has a population of 5,390,576 people. To put that figure into context, the region is home to more people than Scotland, Wales or Ireland. In fact, if it were a country, it would be the 120th most populous of 233 countries on Earth, ahead of nations such as New Zealand, Croatia, Costa Rica, Uruguay and Georgia.

Q is for quoits

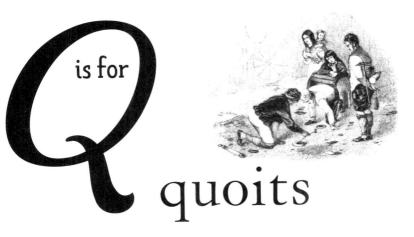

Although its popularity has waned, the game of quoits was once as much a part of life in working-class Yorkshire as football or cricket. It is one of the most ancient games still played in Britain, reputedly dating back to the reign of King John (1199–1216).

In 1829, George Oliver, of Beverley in the East Riding, noted that "the lower classes of people have their quoits, their foot-ball and their cricket". As he set off on his *Month in Yorkshire*, published in 1861, Walter White said he wanted to discover if Northallerton was still famous "for quoits, cricket, and spell-and-nurr" (the latter being another traditional Yorkshire game).

Yorkshire cannot claim to have been the birthplace of quoits (some purists insist the quoit is a variant of the discus and was therefore played at the first Greek Olympiad); however, as with football and rugby, the modern game's roots lie in Yorkshire.

The first known written set of rules were published in *The Field* magazine in 1881 by the Association of Amateur Quoits Clubs for the North of England. These rules formed what is now called The Northern Game and they have remained largely unchanged ever since. The Northern Game continues to be played in parts of Yorkshire – particularly the Dales and the North York Moors – under the auspices of The National Quoits Association.

Fortunately, the distinctive ringing sound of heavy steel rings hitting a metal target pin (often embedded in clay) remains a familiar sound in the villages of North Yorkshire during warm summer evenings.

Q is for

Quality
Street

While York is surely the undisputed Chocolate City, Halifax has long been known as Toffee Town.

It all started back in 1890, when John and Violet Mackintosh bought a pastry shop in Halifax and began selling toffee – a special blend of the traditional, brittle English butterscotch and the soft American caramel.

Sold under the name "Mackintosh's Celebrated Toffee", the company rapidly expanded, such was the popularity of this affordable sweet.

By 1914, John Mackintosh Ltd employed some 1,000 people, with operations in Europe, Australia and Canada.

While toffee was cheap, chocolate remained something of a luxury

The company became famous for its marketing campaigns, which ensured its remarkable success.

After "Toffee King" John Mackintosh's death in 1920, son Harold took over the business and thanks to a string of Heath Robinson cartoons in national newspapers, Halifax became "Toffee Town".

In 1936, Mackintosh's launched perhaps its most iconic brand, Quality

An old Quality Street advertisement featuring the characters Miss Sweetly and Major Quality

Did you know?

6,000 Quality Street sweets are produced per minute, a total of 67 million every week

Street. It revolutionised the way confectionery was manufactured and sold.

While toffee was cheap – manufactured from local ingredients such as milk, sugar and eggs – chocolate remained something of a luxury.

By combining toffee with chocolate, Mackintosh's was able to make it affordable for working families.

Back then, Quality Street cost two shillings, equivalent to £3.69 in today's money.

Alex Hutchinson, heritage assistant for Nestlé UK – the present-day owners of Quality Street – explained, "At the beginning of the 1930s, before Quality Street was invented, boxed chocolates were very expensive. Only wealthy people could afford them. They contained exotic ingredients from around the world and were sold in elaborate packaging that cost just as much as the contents."

To bring costs down, the company used groundbreaking technology such as the world's first twist-wrapping machine to create one of the most colourful and enticing products available in the mass market. It coated the cheaper toffee in chocolate and packaged the sweets in brightly coloured tins, decorated inside with bunting and ribbons, and sold them at a reasonable price.

As ever with Mackintosh's, marketing was key. The name, a pun on "quality sweet", was inspired by a play of the same name by JM Barrie of *Peter Pan* fame.

Quality Street chocolates have been a Christmas favourite for decades

Did you know?

Around thirty per cent of the Quality Street made in the UK is exported to seventy countries, including France, Denmark and Canada

Did you know?

Tins and advertisements featured two characters, Miss Sweetly and Major Quality, who were based on the main characters in the play.

"Mackintosh knew that in times of economic hardship and war, people crave nostalgia," explained Miss Hutchinson.

"Britain was still feeling the effects of the economic crash at the beginning of the decade and power was shifting in Europe. Consumers wanted to be reminded of a more reliable, bygone era."

As had been customary, Quality Street was launched with a huge advertising blitz. The whole of page one of the *Daily Mail* was bought up to announce its arrival.

Every aspect of the new sweets was carefully considered. "Quality Street was designed to be an entirely new, multi-sensory experience," explained Miss Hutchinson. "By using a tin box, instead of a cardboard one, Mackintosh ensured the scents wafted out as soon as you opened it. The different textures, colours, shapes and sizes of the sweets made opening the tin and consuming its contents a noisy, vibrant experience that the whole family could enjoy."

Quality Street was an immediate success and it continued to grow, becoming the world's number one-selling boxed chocolate assortment.

The selection changed down the years, with sweets such as the Hazelnut Cracknell, Gooseberry Cream and Apricot Delight among the discontinued varieties. Major and Miss remained on the packaging until 2000.

In 1969 the company merged with Rowntree's to form Rowntree Mackintosh and in 1988, that company was taken over by Nestlé.

However, Quality Street is still produced in Halifax and it continues to innovate, bringing out specially designed tins for special occasions. Since 2009, the packaging has been completely recyclable.

R is for **rain**

Y ou could be forgiven for thinking it rains rather a lot in Yorkshire. You'd be wrong. In fact, the county is one of the driest parts of Britain. Its average rainfall of 32.6 inches (82.8cm) each year is only just above the national average of 33 inches (83.8cm). Yorkshire has just over half as much rain as Scotland, and the North West receives a third more precipitation.

R is for rhubarb

Yorkshire's slightly less tropical answer to the Bermuda Triangle is the Rhubarb Triangle. A nine-square-mile area of land between the holy trinity of Wakefield, Morley and Rothwell benefits from perfect conditions for growing rhubarb. The fact that rhubarb is a native of Siberia is a clue to the plant's preferred climate.

The soils of the area have also been improved over the decades with the addition of manure and by-products of West Yorkshire industry.

67

Once upon a time, West Yorkshire produced a remarkable ninety per cent of the world's winter forced rhubarb.

Yorkshire forced rhubarb is still grown in sheds using traditional methods. Rhubarb pickers pull the stalks by candlelight as any exposure to strong light stunts the plant's growth.

The rhubarb of the region is said to sprout so fast that if you listen hard enough, you can actually hear it growing.

When the industry was at its peak in the late nineteenth century, "rhubarb special" express trains were run from Ardsley Station every weekday night between Christmas and Easter, carrying tonnes of rhubarb from the West Riding to London.

A sculpture in Wakefield celebrates the so-called "Rhubarb Triangle" of Wakefield, Rothwell and Morley

West Yorkshire once produced ninety per cent of the world's winter forced rhubarb

Having dipped out of favour after the Second World War, when more exotic fruits became available, rhubarb is back in fashion again. Some of Britain's best-known chefs incorporate rhubarb into their recipes and most insist on it coming from the Rhubarb Triangle. Forced rhubarb is more tender than that grown outdoors in the summer.

R is for *Ridings*

Yorkshire is historically split into three Ridings – North, East and West, plus the City of York. There has never been a South Riding, though confusingly a novel of that name, by Winifred Holtby, was published in 1936. Her inspiration was the East Riding rather than South Yorkshire.

The word comes from the old Norse *thrithjungr*, which became, in Old English, *thridding*. It means simply "a third part".

There could be no fourth Riding because the word comes from the old Norse *thrithjungr*, which became, in Old English, *thridding*. It means simply "a third part". The invading Danes established the Ridings system as a way of governing the region.

Although the Ridings name was dropped during local government organisation in 1974, groups such as the Yorkshire Ridings Society campaign to protect the ancient boundaries. A declaration read in each of the three Ridings every Yorkshire Day states that "any person or corporate body which ignores or denies" the Ridings of Yorkshire "shall forfeit all claim to Yorkshire status".

R is for Robin Hood

Modern retellings of the legend link Robin Hood with Sherwood Forest and the city of Nottingham, resulting in a tourism boon for those areas. However, the outlaw's links with Yorkshire seem far stronger.

The court records of the York Assizes of 12th July, 1225, refer to one Robert Hod, fugitive. A year later he was referred to again, this time as "Robinhud", with a bounty of thirty-two shillings and sixpence.

The earliest medieval ballads of Robin Hood state the outlaw lives in Barnsdale Forest, between Pontefract and Doncaster, South Yorkshire. In "Robin Hood and Guy of Gisborne", Robin says: "My name is Robin Hood of Barnesdale, A fellow thou has long sought." Indeed, in only one of the medieval ballads is Sherwood Forest mentioned.

The hero is often referred to as Robin of Loxley, suggesting that his birthplace is Loxley, now a suburb of Sheffield.

Several accounts name Kirklees, twenty miles west of Barnsdale, as the location of Robin's death and burial. Robin Hood's Grave, a monument in the Kirklees Park Estate, marks the spot.

Ridley Scott's 2010 film *Robin Hood* tried to right some of the wrongs.

S is for saucy

I s Yorkshire England's sauciest county? It certainly has a strong case. Firstly, the wonderfully spicy, delightfully fruity Henderson's Relish has been made in Sheffield for more than 100 years. Then there's the doyen of the saucy novel, Jilly Cooper, who grew up in Ilkley. Yorkshire also produced the Calendar Girls, the ladies of Rylstone & District WI, who shed their clothes for a charity calendar and raised millions of pounds (and several pulse rates) in the process.

Racy novel queen Jilly Cooper, a native of Ilkley, with her cat in 1974

Yorkshire brought the world the saucy seaside postcard

But the clincher is that Yorkshire brought the world the saucy seaside postcard.

In 1910, Bamforth & Co of Holmfirth – previously a respected photography and filmmaking business – came up with the idea of cheeky illustrated postcards.

The concept took off and before long business was booming. Sales of saucy seaside postcards exploded, thanks to their bawdy humour laden with innuendo and double entendre.

At their peak in the 1930s, an incredible sixteen million were sold each year.

But in the '50s, the government became concerned the cards were symptomatic of a decline in the nation's moral standards and there was a crackdown on the sauciest of the cards, under the powers of the Obscene Publications Act 1857. The business took a real hit.

At their peak in the 1930s, an incredible sixteen million of the cards were sold each year

In the more liberal 1960s and '70s, the postcards came back into fashion until declining once more in the 1980s. Bamforth's was eventually sold to West Yorkshire businessman Ian Wallace and on the 100th anniversary of the invention of the saucy postcard, in 2010, the firm once more began publishing and selling its risqué cards. The sauce had been put back into Yorkshire's bottle.

Deliciously saucy Henderson's Relish, which has been made in Sheffield for over 100 years

is for

T tea

Surely Harrogate, North Yorkshire, must be Britain's tea capital. It is home to one of the world's most famous tearooms (Bettys) and one of the UK's most successful tea producers (Yorkshire Tea). But, the town's love affair with tea began relatively recently. Historically the town was much better known for its water, unsullied by tea leaves. Whisper this quietly but, at one stage, visitors to Harrogate were strongly advised to avoid tea because of its "pernicious" side-effects.

In *A Treatise on the Mineral Waters of Harrogate*, published in 1810, Thomas Garnett stated, "The best drink during dinner is pure water. For breakfast, milk, chocolate, or cocoa, will be much better than tea, which in nervous complaints, and weakened and relaxed stomachs, is always improper; but besides the pernicious effects of tea, upon such constitutions, its use is highly improper for those who are drinking the chalybeate waters." He added, "If a little infusion of tea be mixed with any of the chalybeate waters, the mixture assumes a purple colour" and even claimed that tea "must destroy, or at least lessen the good effects expected" from Harrogate's mineral waters.

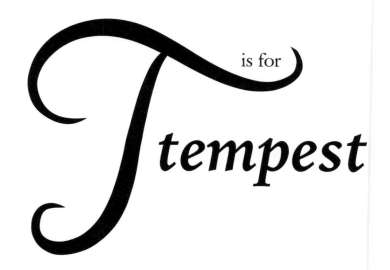

is for

tempest

A s we have already discussed, it doesn't always rain in Yorkshire – but from time to time, the county is hit by some pretty severe storms. One of the worst struck in 1686. It was described in one history book as a "tempest, accompanied with thunder, which committed general devastation". Particularly badly affected were two villages in the Yorkshire Dales, where virtually every resident was killed.

It was described as a "tempest, accompanied with thunder, which committed general devastation"

"The inhabitants of Kettlewell and Starbotton, in Craven, were almost all drowned in a violent flood," according to one account. "These villages are situate under a great hill, whence the rain descended with such violence for an hour and a half, that the hill on one side opened, and casting up water into the air to the height of an ordinary church steeple, demolished several houses, and carried away the stones entirely."

T is for

tyke

Once used as an insult against Yorkshire folk, the term "tyke" is now accepted and owned by the county's residents – particularly in the West Riding. It is now both a nickname for a Yorkshireman and a name for the county's dialect.

The word is said to originate from the Old Norse *tík*, meaning female dog or bitch. It is possible the historic link with Yorkshire is thanks to the terrier that was widely bred and owned in the county.

Barnsley FC have adopted the term as their nickname and the Tyke's Motto has for decades been reproduced on tea-towels, mugs and plaques. It goes as follows:

> *'Ear all, see all, say nowt;*
> *Eat all, sup all, pay nowt;*
> *And if ivver tha does owt fer nowt*
> *Allus do it fer thissen.*

Is Yorkshire's native terrier at the root of the nickname "tyke"?

U is for underwear

Although the stereotype would have you believe that the Yorkshireman is conservative and no-nonsense, when it comes to his choice of underwear it transpires the truth is somewhat different.

In the 1930s, Britain was lagging behind America in the undies stakes. While new, more flattering, athletic styles and fabrics were being popularised across the Atlantic, British men were sticking stubbornly to the old Victorian and Edwardian styles. Except, that is, in Yorkshire.

Miners favoured "short cotton knickers shaped much like a pair of running shorts, but not so full"

In 1930, *Men's Wear* magazine criticised the UK underwear trade for perpetuating the view that British men "don't want such things as rayon vests and elastic-waisted shorts". It insisted there was demand for new, more minimalist and comfortable pants.

The publication noted that Yorkshire miners, working deep underground, favoured "short cotton knickers shaped much like a pair of running shorts, but not so full". *Men's Wear* reported that these were being bought by local youngsters to be worn as underwear. True trendsetters.

V *is for* *vampire*

The most famous vampire of them all may have been a Transylvanian but his bloodline can be traced directly back to Yorkshire. The fishing port of Whitby provided writer Bram Stoker with atmospheric locations for his most famous novel – and a name for his lead character.

Stoker arrived in Whitby in the summer of 1890. He was looking for some rest and recuperation following a gruelling theatre tour of Scotland.

On 8th August 1890, Stoker strolled along to the town's public library and picked up a book published seventy years earlier, recounting the experiences of a British consul in Bucharest. The tome described a fifteenth-century prince called Vlad Ţepeş who was said to have impaled his enemies on wooden stakes. He was also known as Dracula, "son of the dragon". A footnote added: "Dracula in the Wallachian language means Devil. The Wallachians at that time … used to give this as a surname to any person who rendered himself conspicuous either by courage, cruel actions, or cunning." Stoker eagerly jotted down the name. And so *Dracula* was born.

While *Dracula* was a complete work of fiction, could it be that Yorkshire was once also home to real-life vampires? In the far west of the county, in the village of Dent, can be found a gravestone marking the death, in 1715, of George Hodgson.

Hodgson died at the then-remarkable age of ninety-four. Rumour locally had it

Above: Bram Stoker, author of *Dracula*, in 1906; Opposite: ruinous Whitby Abbey remains a pilgrimage site for fans of the novel; Below: Vlad the Impaler

that Hodgson's longevity was because of a pact he had made with the Devil. One "friend" even claimed he had enjoyed a daily glass of sheep's blood.

Not long after his burial, in a quiet corner of the churchyard, there were reports that people had begun seeing Hodgson walking in the moonlit graveyard – worse still, each witness was said to have died shortly after seeing this terrifying apparition.

Following a meeting of local residents it is said his body was exhumed and when the coffin was opened his hair and nails had grown and his flesh was glowing pink, as though he were still alive.

The corpse was promptly reburied next to the church porch, with a brass stake driven through his corpse, to bring an end to his moonlit excursions.

Visitors to Dent churchyard can still see what appears to be a hole drilled through his gravestone and what remains of the stake. However, some cynics have suggested it is more likely to be what was used as part of a fixing mechanism to keep the porch gate in place.

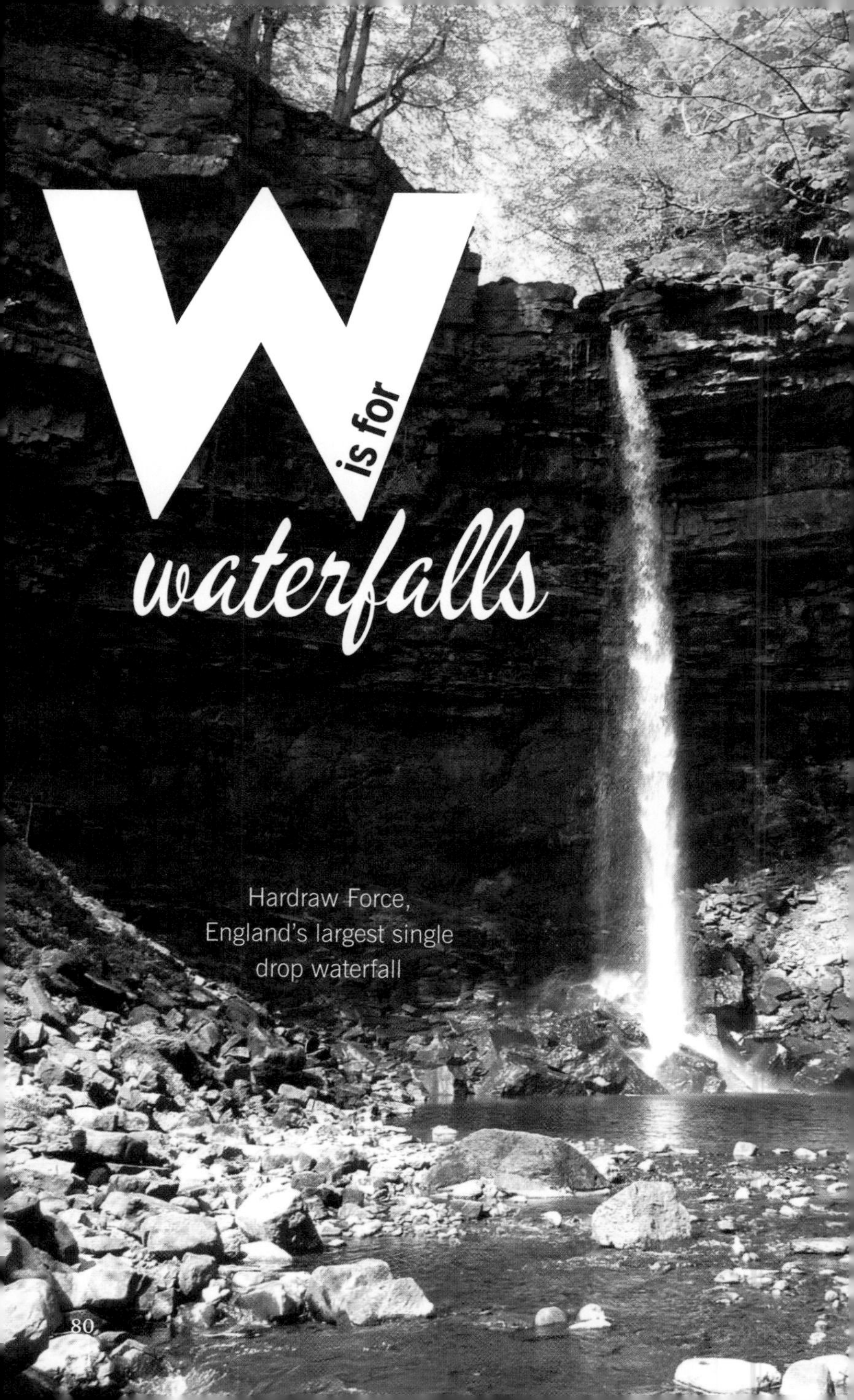

W
is for
waterfalls

Hardraw Force,
England's largest single
drop waterfall

Yorkshire is England's waterfall county. It boasts England's largest single drop waterfall – Hardraw Force, the single drop waterfall with the highest volume of water – High Force and the highest unbroken waterfall above or below ground, Gaping Gill. However, all records could have been smashed had plans to create an artificial waterfall in the Yorkshire Dales been approved.

"In great floods," wrote Thomas Dugdale in 1830, "the waters above Malham Cove form an immense cataract, superior in height to the falls of Niagara".

It is a sight rarely witnessed. On Sunday, 6th December 2015, the waterfall briefly returned to the limestone cliff for the first time in decades. Yet, had ambitious plans been given the go-ahead, water could have flowed over Malham Cove in perpetuity.

An audacious scheme was mooted in 1899 when Skipton MP and owner of the Malham Tarn estate Walter Morrison received a letter from a correspondent who "thought that it might be possible, by constructing a leak-proof channel from the foot of Malham Tarn to the edge of Malham Cove to recreate what is referred to by Dugdale as... 'an immense cataract superior to the Falls of Niagara'." The MP replied that "a waterfall over the cove would spoil it as a landscape".

The idea was not sunk forever, however. In July 1926, the Rev Charles Tweedale, vicar of Weston, near Otley, proposed creating a "waterfall that would be the highest in England". He argued that rather than being a once-in-a-generation spectacle, "this grand natural phenomenon might be made permanent by simply blocking up the surface fissures at the two points near Coom Scar, or by diverting the channel of the stream at these points."

Residents of nearby Malham dismissed it as a "joke". One report declared they "refuse to take seriously" the proposal and "seem amused at the idea, as well as sceptical as to its practicability".

Writing in the Malhamdale parish magazine, the Rev W R N Baron claimed, "It would swallow up Malham village and would involve puddling a good many hundred acres to keep the water from siping through the limescale."

Rev Tweedale was not to be put off, however, insisting, "Such trivial objections and fears should not be allowed to stand in the way of the realisation of a notable addition to the interest and beauty of one of the most romantic districts in this country and the creating of the highest waterfall in England."

All records could have been smashed had plans to create an artificial waterfall in the Yorkshire Dales been approved

The unlikely scheme resurfaced once more, in 1931, when a parish meeting was held in Malham to discuss the idea. The proposal was then discussed by Settle Rural Council. In a letter to the authority, the Society for the Preservation of Rural England called the plans "disgusting theatricalism", adding "the waterfall would be ridiculous in relation to its surroundings." And with that rebuke, the plans to create England's answer to Niagara sank without trace.

The Rev Tweedale died in June 1929, and he ended his life making headlines once more. "When Father died we expected his return," Miss Tweedale told the *Yorkshire Post*. "Evidently he has come back to show us he is all right."

His widow and his youngest daughter, Dorothy, said that "he returned in spiritual form, with a host of friends" including Sir Arthur Conan Doyle and Chopin.

Miss Tweedale said the manifestation took place in the dining room in the early hours of the Saturday after the vicar's death.

"There was a brilliant light at the side of the room, ectoplasm began to swirl in clouds and then Stradivarius, the famous violin maker" – a 'spirit friend' of the Tweedales for many years – "appeared in head and shoulder form. A little afterwards my father appeared, first as a man in his prime, then as he was before he died."

The manifestation, they said, lasted at least an hour and "during it British soldiers in khaki and steel helmets, whom they thought were men who had just died, formed what seemed like a guard of honour."

Malham Cove could have been the site of "England's Niagara" (artist's impression)

W is for White Rose

The White Rose of York is the symbol of the House of York that has been adopted as a symbol of the whole county. More recently it has been incorporated into the county's flag, placed on a blue background.

The origins of the emblem are not certain, though they are said to date back to the fourteenth century, pre-dating the Wars of the Roses. The Red Rose of Lancaster was a later invention not in use at the time of the actual conflict.

At the Battle of Minden on 1st August 1759, members of the King's Own Yorkshire Light Infantry's predecessor, the 51st Regiment, picked white roses from bushes near to the battlefields, sticking them to their coats as a tribute to their fallen comrades. For this reason, Yorkshire Day is held on this date each year.

There is some confusion as to which way up the Yorkshire rose should be displayed. The answer, it seems, depends on where you are in Yorkshire. According to the College of Heralds, the heraldic rose can be used with either a petal or a sepal at the top. And the Yorkshire Ridings Society states: "There is a tradition of using the rose with a petal at the top in the North Riding and the West Riding but with a sepal at the top in the East Riding."

W is for Wonderland

S o many aspects of Lewis Carroll's most famous work are said to have been inspired by locations in Yorkshire that the county can surely lay claim to being the real Wonderland. As a headline in *The Independent* declared in 2000, "It was really Alice in Yorkshireland".

For years, Oxford, Daresbury in Cheshire and Llandudno, North Wales, have built whole tourism industries around *Alice's Adventures in Wonderland*, but Yorkshire's influence is not so well-known.

A rabbit carved into the stonework of St Mary's, Beverley, is said to have inspired Carroll in his creation of the tardy White Rabbit. The writer is believed to have seen the bunny, carrying a messenger bag, scroll and staff, during a family outing to Beverley. Another theory argues the rabbit was in fact based upon a carving in Ripon Cathedral, where Carroll's father was canon. One depicts a rabbit escaping down a hole. Another shows a griffin, perhaps the Gryphon from *Through the Looking Glass*. A third shows odd-looking little creatures with their faces in their bodies, just as Carroll imagined Alice when she had shrunk.

There is also a theory that four-year-old Ripon girl Mary Badcock was more of an inspiration for Alice than Alice Liddell, the child Carroll knew at Oxford. She is said to have been the photographic model for Sir John Tenniel's illustration of Alice. Mary lived at Ure Lodge, Ripon, where, in 1834, a hole sixty-five feet (20m) deep suddenly opened up in the ground. Subsidence is a long-standing problem in Ripon, which stands above a large system of gypsum caves. Large subsidence holes regularly appear and one of these could very easily have inspired Alice's fall below ground for what was originally entitled *Alice's Adventures Under Ground*.

Above: the rabbit carving at St Mary's Church, Beverley, may have inspired the ever-tardy White Rabbit (opposite); Below: detail from the griffin misericord at Ripon Cathedral that may have been the inspiration for *Looking Glass*'s Gryphon

As a headline in *The Independent* declared in 2000, "It was really Alice in Yorkshireland"

Another Yorkshire town with strong Wonderland connections is Whitby. Carroll visited the seaside town on six occasions between 1854 and 1898, and it was here that his earliest works were published. Local newspaper the *Whitby Gazette* printed his satirical poem "The

Lady of the Ladle" and a short story, describing the approach to the town. During his early visits to Whitby as a young man, he would take pleasure from reading stories to children. Dr Thomas Fowler, who was in attendance, recalled that Carroll "used to sit on a rock on the beach telling stories to a circle of eager young listeners of both sexes", and he believed that "it was there that *Alice* was incubated".

Locals believe the Caucus Race in Wonderland may have been inspired by races Carroll organised to help young day-trippers dry out after a sudden rain-shower. They also say the Walrus and the Carpenter could have been inspired by Whitby's beach.

The Walrus and the Carpenter could have been inspired by Whitby's beach

The Yorkshire connections don't end there. One of Carroll's childhood homes was in Croft-on-Tees, a village in the northern borderlands of Yorkshire, where it is said that he penned the first verse of "Jabberwocky". Here, in the church that stands just yards from his home, there is a carving of a grinning animal. It's a dead ringer for Carroll's Cheshire Cat.

X-Files

X is for

From big cats on Ilkley Moor to strange lights above Holmfirth, Yorkshire has had more than its fair share of other-worldly activities down the years. Yorkshire's bulging X-Files would have kept paranormal investigators Mulder and Scully busy for years.

Perhaps the strangest of all is the case of local Labour councillor Simon Parkes, of Whitby, who claimed in 2012 that he had been adopted as a baby by a nine-foot tall green alien, who explained that she was his "real, more important mother".

The Guardian reported: "Later, when he was eleven, she took him on board her spacecraft and a deal was stuck about contact between the two worlds."

In a video he posted on YouTube, Parkes recalled seeing his alien mother as a baby in his cot: "Two green stick things came in. I was aware of some movement over my head. I thought, 'they're not Mummy's hands, Mummy's hands are pink'. I was looking straight into its face. It enters my mind through my eyes and it sends a message down my optic nerve into my brain. It says 'I am your real mother, I am your more important mother.'"

The Whitby Town Council member added that his alien connections don't hamper his job. "It's a personal matter and it doesn't affect my work. I'm more interested in fixing someone's leaking roof or potholes. People don't want me to talk about aliens."

However, he did also say: "I get more common sense out of the aliens than out of Scarborough Town Hall. The aliens are far more aware of stuff. People in the town hall seem not to be aware of the needs of Whitby."

He has since claimed he has fathered a child called Zarka with an extraterrestrial he refers to as the Cat Queen.

The truth is out there.

Do aliens lurk on
Ilkley Moor?

For years, rail passengers arriving at York Station were greeted by a giant billboard that read "Welcome to York: Where the Men are Hunky and the Chocolate is Chunky!" From its earliest days, chocolatier Rowntree was proud of its roots, using "York" in the name of several confectionery products and pictures of the city in marketing and packaging. Early Rowntree chocolate tins featured York Minster and the Rose of York, while one of the company's first brands was Rowntree's York Chocolates, an assortment box carrying the York seal, which was made in the city until the outbreak of the First World War. Production never restarted after the war; instead, in 1925, Rowntree launched Plain York eating chocolate using the advertising slogan, "I'm Plain Mr York of York, Yorks", which deliberately repeated the brand name three times for emphasis. It was a big success for the company and it was followed in 1928 by the York Milk, which was sold in squares and bars.

Rowntree struggled to challenge the dominance of Cadbury in the milk chocolate bar market, and concentrated on other products, such as the KitKat and Fruit Pastilles. Cadbury's Dairy Milk seemed untouchable for decades, as its rivals looked on enviously. However, in the 1960s and '70s, cocoa prices soared – between 1973 and 1977, for instance, prices increased tenfold. Cadbury was concerned that sales would be hit if it increased the price of the Dairy Milk chocolate bar above the one shilling threshold. Instead, it gradually reduced the weight and thickness of the bar. Rowntree Mackintosh, as it was now called, carried out customer research in the mid-1970s which showed that the public was unhappy with the shrinking Cadbury bars. Consumers, they found, preferred chunkier chocolate – and they would be willing to pay more for it. The result, in 1976, was the Yorkie bar. Its name, like that of Plain York and York Milk, celebrated Rowntree's home city.

An advertisement for Plain York chocolate featuring "Plain Mr York of York, Yorks"

The marketing deliberately focused on the "manly" size of the chocolate chunks

After a successful trial in the North East of England, Yorkie was launched nationwide, with a high-profile advertising campaign that featured a lorry driver chomping on the new bars. The marketing deliberately focused on the "manly" size of the chocolate chunks. The result was immediate. Rowntree's market research had been spot on. There was a real public appetite for the chunkier bars and the scale of the success of the Yorkie juggernaut stunned Cadbury, and possibly even Rowntree too. In what was one of the most successful British product launches of all time, Yorkie took a huge chunk of the market from Cadbury. By 1978, Yorkie's annual sales volume had reached 13,000 tonnes – double the amount achieved by any new Cadbury product since the war. Cadbury now had less than half of the moulded chocolate category, which it had invented and shaped. Cadbury responded that year by introducing a new, chunkier mould, but Yorkie had the upper hand.

One of the Yorkie creators, Eric Nicoli, explained recently, "The chunky chocolate block was so superior because Cadbury's had slimmed down their blocks to cope with the rising cost of cocoa. Before long, Rowntree's Yorkie had gone from zero to forty-five per cent of the market while Cadbury's share had fallen from eighty per cent to thirty-five per cent."

The lorry driver was the rough, tough star of Yorkie adverts for sixteen years until 1992. Then, after a break in advertising, in 2002 Yorkie was relaunched under the controversial slogan, "It's not for girls". In 2006, a limited edition bar, in pink, went on sale, with the slogan "Girls, can you handle it?". Then, in 2012, a new, similarly macho tagline, "Man Fuel for Man Stuff", was introduced. Ironically, given the reason for its invention, Yorkie has been criticised recently after it shrank in size twice in only three years, while the cost of cocoa tumbled; leading one newspaper to declare it's "no longer man-sized".

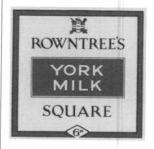

Rowntree was proud of its roots, using "York" in the name of several products as well as pictures of the city in packaging

Z is for zebra crossing

It was a modest and largely anonymous Yorkshireman who first introduced black and white stripes to pedestrian crossings, subsequently saving countless lives and giving the world one of its most iconic album covers.

George Charlesworth was born in 1917 in Elslack, a pretty little hamlet near Skipton, on the edge of the Yorkshire Dales. As a young physicist he had worked on the Barnes Wallis-designed bouncing bombs used in the Dambusters raid on Germany's Ruhr Valley. But it was in his later career as a traffic engineer that he would truly change the world.

Charlesworth always refused to take credit for inventing the zebra crossing, insisting it was a team effort. However, the crossing was the result of work under his direction, and as the stripes became commonplace across Britain's roads, Charlesworth became fondly known as Dr Zebra.

The origin of the name "zebra crossing" is disputed, but the most common theory is that when MP and future prime minister James Callaghan visited the offices of the Transport Research Laboratory in 1948, he remarked that the design resembled a zebra.

One problem with this theory is that the first 1,000 of Charlesworth's crossings, introduced in 1949, were in fact painted blue and yellow. It was only two years later, when the project was rolled out nationwide, that the distinctive black and white was adopted, to increase their visibility at night. Zebra crossings are now commonplace across the world. Probably the most famous appears on the cover of The Beatles' *Abbey Road* album.

Z is for

Zzzz...

nd finally, Yorkshire is home to many things – as this book has hopefully proved – but I'll bet you didn't know it is also the official home of sleep.

It all started in 1807 when William Sharp, a weaver from Laycock, near Keighley, went to bed and stayed there for the rest of his life.

The headquarters of national agency The Sleep Council are based in Skipton, North Yorkshire

A regular at the Devonshire in Keighley, the young Sharp fell in love with the barmaid there. He proposed, she accepted and they were to be married. However, when the big day came, the girl jilted the unfortunate Sharp at the altar. He was devastated, and "went to bed and never rose from it again". He refused to speak to anyone and never even opened his bedroom window.

Old Three Laps, as he was known, became famous far and wide. The *Preston Chronicle* in 1839 described him as "rolled up like a hedgehog", adding that his beard was "grisly, his hair silvery white, and most enormous teeth project from his lips". The 1851 census described him as: "Unmarried. Aged 74. Independent Landed Proprietor. Lain in bed 44 years".

He died in 1856, after spending almost fifty years between the sheets.

Just twelve miles from Laycock you will find the gloriously named village of Idle. Visitors delight in photographing the sign above the door of Idle Working Men's Club (pictured below).

Another much-photographed sign can be found in the East Riding of Yorkshire, where motorists are directed towards the Land of Nod. This is not the spot mentioned in the Old Testament, or even the mythical place we go to when we sleep, but a tiny hamlet situated at the end of a narrow two-mile road, near Holme-on-Spalding-Moor.

And if that's not making you feel sleepy enough, the headquarters of national agency The Sleep Council are located in Skipton, North Yorkshire. According to its website: "The Sleep Council is an impartial organisation that looks at how you can adopt healthier sleep habits and focuses on raising awareness of a good night's sleep to health and wellbeing." In 2013 the council produced the *Great British Bedtime Report*. Among the revelations contained within were the findings that the highest earners sleep best while those on the lowest incomes sleep worst; and the average Briton goes to bed at 11.15pm.

Night, night.

Picture credits

Ale (cover) © padmasanjaya; zebra (cover, p5) © idesign2000; flat cap (p5) © tashanatasha; beer (pp6–7) © weyo; George Cayley glider replica (p8) © Nigel Coates: CC BY-SA 3.0; George Cayley (p9): public domain; George Cayley glider diagram (p9): public domain; John Wycliffe Bible (p10) © Denysmonroe81: CC BY-SA 3.0; detail from Wycliffe Bible (p11): public domain; Battle of Towton (p12): public domain; swastika stone (p13) © David Spencer: CC BY-SA 2.0; bauble (p14): FreeImages.com/John De Boer; turkey (p14) © Dinner Series: CC BY 2.0; cartoon cat (p16) © freedesignfile; cat's eye (p16): public domain; cat's eye poster (p18): Reflecting Roadstuds Ltd; drystone wall (p19): Adrian Braddy; Devil's Arrows (p20) © Fog76: CC BY-SA 3.0; Devil's Arrows blue plaque (p21) © Benjamin Shaw: CC BY-SA 3.0; Easter Eggs cartoon (p23) © BSGStudio; Pace Egg Play (p23) © Phil Champion: CC BY-SA 2.0; Frances and the Fairies (p25): public domain; cartoon football (p27): www.webdesignhot.com; Sheffield FC crest (p27): Sheffield FC; Thomas Percy, Earl of Northumberland (p28): public domain; 35 Stonegate (p29) © Jhsteel: CC BY-SA 3.0; gunpowder plot (pp30–31): public domain; the Ripon Wakeman's house (p33) © Gordon Hatton: CC BY-SA 2.0; The King's Speech (p34) © www.lancashire.gov.uk: CC BY 2.0; King's speech dummies (p35) © University of Huddersfield; Whitby jet (p36): public domain; Camelot (p37): public domain; Kiplingcotes Derby finishing post (p39) © Ian Lavender: CC BY-SA 2.0; The Leech Finders (p40): public domain; leech jar (p41): Wellcome Library, London; medicinal leech diagram (p42): Wellcome Library, London; the leech house (p43) © Rosser1954: CC BY-SA 4.0; Salts Mill (p44) © Tim Green: CC BY 2.0; Armley Mills (p45) © Chris Allen: CC BY-SA 2.0; Little Nipper mousetrap (p46) © Jerry mouse: CC BY-SA 3.0; Mother Shipton's Cave (p47) © chris 論: CC BY 3.0; Mother Shipton engraving (p48): public domain; Mother Shipton's house (p48): public domain; John Cockcroft (p49): public domain; Owen Willans Richardson (p50): public domain; The Naked Man (p51) © Michael Ely: CC BY-SA 2.0; The Naked Woman (p51) © John Illingworth: CC BY-SA 2.0; Gold postbox (p53) © TerryRobinson: CC BY-SA 2.0; Old Boots (p54): public domain; Yorkshire puddings (p56) © FomaA; Foster Powell (p57): Wellcome Library, London; Charles Watson-Wentworth (p59): public domain; Herbert Henry Asquith (p59): public domain; quoits (p61): public domain; Quality Streets (p62) © Alex Brown Flickr: CC BY-SA 2.0; Quality Street advertisement (p63): Nestlé UK Archives; Quality Street advertisement (p64): Nestlé UK Archives; umbrella (p66): FreeImages.com/juri Staikov; rhubarb (p67): FreeImages.com/Michael & Christa Richert; rhubarb sculpture (p68) © Mike Kirby: CC BY-SA 2.0; Robin Hood (p70): public domain; Jilly Cooper (p71) © Allan Warren: CC BY-SA 3.0; Henderson's Relish (p72) © Andy Dingley: CC BY-SA 3.0; teapot cartoon (p73) © Amili; Yorkshire terrier (p75) © Gandalfelrojo2: CC BY-SA 4.0; underwear (p76): public domain; vampire (p77): public domain; Bram Stoker (p78): public domain; Vlad the Impaler (p78): public domain; Whitby Abbey (p79) © Chris Kirk: CC BY 2.0; Hardraw Force (p80) © Wehha: CC BY-SA 3.0; Malham Falls (p82) © Dalesman; White Rose (p84): CC BY-SA 3.0; Alice (p85): public domain; rabbit carving (p86): public domain; griffin carving (p86) © David Iliff: CC-BY-SA 3.0; White Rabbit (p87): public domain; alien on Ilkley Moor (p89) © Dalesman/Pixel77; Yorkie logo (p90): Nestlé; Yorkie bar (p90): Nestlé; Plain York advertisement (p91): Nestlé UK Archives; Rowntrees York Chocolates advertisement (p92): Nestlé UK Archives; Rowntrees York Milk Square advertisement (p92): Nestlé UK Archives; sleeping cartoon (p94) © Alex Hliv; Idle Working Men's Club (p95) © Tim Green: CC BY 2.0.